MINE
ECLOGUE

Mine Eclogue
Jacob Kahn

ROOF BOOKS
New York

ISBN 978-1-7379703-6-1

LIBRARY OF CONGRESS CONTROL NUMBER 2022943806

COVER ART "Facing the Other Side" (detail), by David Wilson

DESIGN Justin Carder

This book is made possible, in part, by the New York State Council on the Arts with the support of the Office of the Governor and the New York State Legislature.

Roof Books
are published by
Segue Foundation
300 Bowery #2, New York, NY 10012
seguefoundation.com

Roof Books
are distributed by
Small Press Distribution
1341 Seventh Street
Berkeley, CA 94710-1403
800-869-7553 or spdbooks.org

CONTENTS

Eclogue I: Ownership Links Arms   11
Sylvan Ditty   12
Eclogue II: Deepwater Horizon   16
Solicitor General   17
Top Result Eclogue   19
Spoonfed Worldview   21
Edge of Water, Västerby Storträsket, Finland   23
Temporary Summons   25
Eclogue III: Alternate Strains   26
Agrarian Capitalism   28
Ragweed Discourages Begonia   30
Telos Is a Feature   31
Eclogue IV: Blood-Soaked Vision   33
A Is for Aegis   36
≠   38
Solvency vs. Liquidity   40
Eclogue V: To Love to Redound   45
Crystal Geyser   46
What Is the Seed Grail?   52
Unaware Fiction   53
Lowest Common Denominator   55
Encomia   56
Frontend Concept + Backend Design   57
Eclogue VI: Automatic Cancellation   58
The Middle Ages   60
Horace   63
I Make the Loose Tooth Friends   65
Eclogue VII: Hack Your Life   66
City Lights   67
Rapidly Reversible Tattoo   69
Arrival   70
Goodnight Moon   71

Antiquity and Onomatopoeia   72

Eclogue VIII: No-Filter Malfeasance   75

Telluric   76

Flat Earth Theory   78

Permian Disappearance   81

Kevin, Come Back   83

Eclogue: Reprise   85

Eclogue IX: Microfiche   90

Deep Space Ballot   91

Direct Deposit   92

Burdensome Organ   93

Canto   94

Eclogue X: Dunk On My Face   95

The Deserts of Saturn   96

Acknowledgments   101

MINE ECLOGUE

It is not possible to make one story out of these two poems, and we must accept that Virgil was not primarily interested in giving us an account of his own experience. These are scenes from the evictions: this sort of thing is going on, and it is tragic.
—Jasper Griffin, Virgil

Eclogue I: Ownership Links Arms

Ever felt happy just to lilt regardless
of the chorus lost to history during
financial crises? Lilt and so will I
feed on splits & throes
loose ere
at the edge of definition

Meanwhile the night air
rises like the perfect excuse
I was happy to feel
in all seriousness
at what mileage
make of me
a forum-dwelling obsessive
(as in face
w/out a motive)
in the sinking light of history
bundled
the currency with the shells

Ever notice Spanish
bayonet in bloom on the desert
looks a whole lot like
beargrass shooting up in
the woods? Lilt and bitter
mites come to mind, slurping rasa
from a leftfielder's glove

doll with eyes closed
solid indignation
ownership links arms

Sylvan Ditty

Have you read the Eclogues is
a gauche question I get but have
you read it?? In the first Eclogue, the conversation between
neighboring shepherds is pretty much about
eminent domain, & rogue legalese, a not-so-unfamiliar
policy of what purpose denies use. This
is the long and short of what we call Pastoral:
common plaint cloaked as Sylvan ditty, same
old groans of muse and lease
e.g. whose boyfriend is that? who

gets to keep his pliant stand?? A few years ago
there were those separatists, remember,
the Bundy clan? The brothers who had an
armed standoff with federal agents over
ranching rights on public lands. They were pissed
about gov't regulations and grazing fees
& were soon connected to rightwing
fucks and white supremacists to like
no one's surprise. The standoff lasted a number of weeks
and was one of those stories you weren't
sure whether to laugh at or watch
in total disgust. One dumbass died trying
to evade a roadblock (Dodge Ram,
snowbank, gun shots). The whole
episode was pretty pastoral. An argument
about land use. It could've been

in the Eclogues. In the poem Meliboeus
laments why his plot is being conscripted for some
Augustinian soldier after Augustus' defeat

of Mark Antony's forces for control
of Rome. It's the late
thirties, there's lots going on
but I guess to thank his troops
Octavian is giving them acres apiece
w/ that sacrificial nonchalance so
typical of empire. Standing Rock
anyone? General Mining
Act of 1872?? Meanwhile

the other shepherd Tityrus
just got back from big city Rome
with word he gets to keep his and is
freaking out while
trying to console his friend
w/ classic unsolicited male advice
to basically
make it brief
when asking for money
from that youth for whom
our altars smoke
six times a year
with no strings attached—

I've similarly heard
get straight to the point
where you can toss around the long intractable
phrases that make it feel like obligation.
It's about asset management. Classic.
Meliboeus doesn't buy it. He's more or less
resigned to his fate and mutters
then one of the most vexed lines
ever: "I envy you not the boon
but marvel more!" Other

translations have it read "I don't begrudge
you, rather I wonder at it" or something
like that. I can't read Latin
but still the sentiment makes him
suddenly much more complex and tragic
and breaks the poem open like
a serious pill. *I prithee passing crow*

go wiki Thrace, wiki
Dakota water defenders!!
Last week my mom texted
a picture w/ the caption
great wildflowers in Albion Basin.
Thousands crossed an ocean claiming
misnomer status. Excuse me sir, but
are all your fish full of plastic??
To say things are beautiful but
fucked
Virgil uses phrases like
"crave thirst" or "fate impelled"
or "backward borne." Ergo for
sea salt—"the salt you toss lightly
on asparagus!"

The poem ends with Meliboeus
saying I'll go somewhere crappy
and sing no more songs. Somewhere like
Briton. Classic. It's about refugee
resettlement. Tityrus says let's
at least enjoy one last evening
on this hill. You know the phrase
to have a lease on life? I've heard

whatever you do
go into the distance,
break open the pill.
Just don't eat the artichoke
I want to see it flower.

Eclogue II: Deepwater Horizon

Suffering in a sequence
is called growing old, Alex, a faithless hope
forever entrenched in the moment
or transfixed by its passing

What is *appetite* anyway?
Annoying eating sounds, dedication
to a false promise

Wings
on the urchin, how to explain
I fell upon a fork in the sea
and discarded the gland

and pined for a face
peeled and placed upon my own
powdering my route w/
coal dust as the case
makes its way through courts

As to be at once holier-than-thou
and down on my luck
and walking a weird line to the lagoon

some game, unburdened
by proof, light years ahead
the platform speaks for itself

Solicitor General

Rosy Amish colors make a reef over
Oakland, up and down Mandela
someone scrawled *no illegal dumpling*
and my phlegmatic head nods
haha, I couldn't agree more. Too bad that
street will liquefy. A rich friend gives
me mineral water he says
to soften my stool I imagine
somewhat like a ship backing up
into a busy waterway, all this gross liquid
pooled onto a capsized frisbee, don't
get your hopes up for the
sphincter is querulous
my friend, very effing querulous. A
starch fable, runny testament. What

makes each feel spurned is
unique to its intestines. Peering
at a blue summation of white
somewhere in SFMOMA. Don't stare directly
at the sun said the solicitor general.
That's your job? said Emma. She meant
the *way* you said it. Dead silence. Click
click. Running a comb through caked hair
I cart melons, administer pulleys,
I go court someone's aegis,
hear complaints of ambivalence
like the soft crinkling of a bag.
In the mounting course of
casuistry almost ready to implore that
part of the roof sunk into a trellised

hill. Super tragic, whatever happened.
Truth is, Falcon, I'm less agent
than instrument, all neck and string
like some weird string instrument
that rich friend owns/takes
down from the wall—suddenly the
song's over and no one even cares to
reprise it. Beauty flecks but more slowly
than alert, preserved in umbrage, an
apple that's pliant as fuck, painted
by Rembrandt, or placed in a little
box like a remnant, like something Cornell
did—a hoarder, a creep, and a craftsman.

Top Result Eclogue

Beginning the process of induction by way of reproval

Elmer Williams calls himself the doctor of common sense

At the moment he makes a suction-like static

Don't hate me, he says, hate the algorithm

It's all part of an elaborately constructed far left sex ritual

You dangle an egg from your septum

And try to express yourself as an unconsolidated fan

To visualize slack and then yank on it

Like a dog chasing its tail in mirrors

Like a discrete fun-loving pair of dolphins

Each has its own plot in mind to bear

The long red trees in tune with the sun

I took time off to grieve in Soda Springs

Time out to spawn in the thicket

I took time to sit on a rock on a hill

Coastal pressure, simple fitness

To intend a song is not to sing it

Dodging bats, I'm in the habit of deceiving

My nose is moist

My flavor palate limited to its basest tingling

I live with it

But not happily

"True behavior"

U-locks

A massive breach of addressees

Spoonfed Worldview
for Jean Day

Interest accrues in the spectrum
rental like a chill ooze or
cash that comes out of the eye
listing through the undertow
I ate my brownie and I ate Karin's
treats
        I did find in the freezer
and you were probably saving
for greater occasions
forgive me
then washed our dishes
and got maybe
as high as you can get
spawning a trail
of synonyms "a creek
beneath Kaiser" John
Waters in Mosswood
It crosses my mind
a liquor called Paradigm
to drink in delight
"at the lazy edges of romance"
in hellish climate, against blessed backdrop
of dross doctrine
& weakness thru vapor
the hum of a fridge
Cogito in fine shape
I punch gaps in the nautical
I dream of a book called *People
On The Plane, Without
Children* my friend

might've written
no cop worth his salt
independent of the lab
in sincere bitterness
1989, fall of Rome, a silent atrium
forefending toxic accrual
it's now or never, bloated conch
buy stock or sink
in liquid waste, ambient rudder
why not mesh
beach and boardwalk
load Nash in the Louvre

Edge of Water, Västerby Storträsket, Finland

for Brian Blanchfield

Call this custom *bypass*, a certain
angle for sitting under oaks, trying
to pinch the edges of address

I didn't mean to refuse the licorice
but regularize this rare flank with
conditions equal to having crawled

inside an elder about to be embalmed.
You there, hundreds of you, tossing
old pillows on the flames. What emblem

is this? Circumspection narrows its
focus from tactility to tactility—think:
overlapping greens—I'm aware stiffen

in the built seeming of a signage.
Trees form a sort of guide.
Meantime "laid on a flat boulder

and watched dragonflies." Dark
navy lupines, talismanic depressions. Adnan:
every sentence is a fleeing, a migration,

to write intimately, for the sake
of intimacy, for nothing else,
no one other than. On this day,

drunk under the chestnuts,

slight febreeze of sunlight,
we lift a dozen flags. Knee-deep

in the Baltic, no one could name
the gull, retrofitting outcomes
like a kind of frozen parasite kids

pick up dead with their oars. Heaves
in sight, tern
in sharp arcs, fugitive, slow

rove into day's remainder
I hear the body contains an
image of itself no will can unlock.

Why else come out to the woods?

Temporary Summons

Parceled as to weaken
the feasibility of a given life
you know, how a loon

swallows a pill, selfish
as rare stone? My love
changing back into me

metamorphoses the question:
do dragonflies parry each
summons even after death?

Through narrow channels,
bordered by lichen,
lands on my leg—if a

lie itself is proof—
no such lie intact.

Eclogue III: Alternate Strains

You out-pipe *him?*
—*Virgil, "Eclogue III"*

Damon, Damon, who cares
about cows?? You can fill these
cups with a milkshake. You
know the song? Twining
vervain is a vampire's most known
weakness. You may not know it
but I saw her in Richmond. *You*
saw *Kelis?* Yeah, I saw her sing

Not my shoe size, thanks, threw
my trash where I found it, dinging
in the sunsets of the original

Ok ok
but when's a good time to text past
lovers just because? Brad, call me
I just switched the clothes
a taste of it lingers, blue
with ginger disregard, people like
to caution, that's clear enough, then swim
far from shore with the gulls overhead

Ask yourself was that
orchid larger than life or
were its hyphens blooming
all over Oakland, the sparrow
singing of some present past
sent through a tube

to revamp the tax law
and stir the lemons

Ask yourself what is generally
thought to be a good idea to
gift on earth? A male
figurine exploded

Agrarian Capitalism

On the bad land, the fault was Nature's; but here,
whose fault?
    —Raymond Williams

You loathe conflict but you're at war with the ants
At times a close look can reveal tens of thousands ceaselessly
    circling through the beams
They say you can't hate hate but that doesn't mean you can't
    practice
And the processes of exploitation dissolve into the landscape

For behind any coincidence is a conflict of values
As one spray of the toxic petroleum distillate performs three
    separate but corollary tasks
Keep out, kill at the source, kill on contact
An alteration of landscape through novel stimulus
A footprint of the full effect in air

Still, ants keep arriving from every crack around the bathtub
As a line, a simple abstraction of their labor
Their work seemingly all done for them by a natural order

Except their work is so visible as labor
This endless flow of laborers
Whose very visibility gives rise to a class
Of merchants and lawyers
I go about spraying w/
Imiprothrin and cypermethrin

Out, damned spot!

A moral is to some extent
A measurement, based in experience,
Against which change can be metered

A numb banality you can feel
Late at night as you vape in the Trader Joe's parking lot
The consequence of a long extended metaphor
On your way to purchase another bottle of Raid

Nor would I trust me in a landscape by myself
Among the many more isolable forms and classes
Pressing our rent thumbs atop the ants

But this is the persistent riff of modernity
As insult to the senses
Whose referent has its own stigma
Invented by the melodramatic shepherd
Crying out loud about feudal lords and labor

The base lyric is dispossession
As moral protest is the greatest pleasure of man

Ragweed Discourages Begonia

Regulators come to paradise
sprigs of lavender, lockets of hair
stuff nobody sesames
quite like the superrich

T'was my sweat
on proctor's brow
tossing bread to the birds
at the lake

Fallacy entails a dampened future
Introspection has a limit
I follow the courageous example of the satellite
I'm not one to enter the valley twice

In the dream an owl
planted in the sea
a hill had thought
moving cups into place

bro, will kill us all
the wigeon in cattails,
the carbon in karst
I refuse the spinal transfer

of alternative fact
dream of the substance
nobody else can
bro, will kill us both

Telos Is a Feature

Credible breakage
at the system's apex
deleting lines at a time
I detect ilex, lies

Sound of the wing's trollop
and signs to dissuade

every afternoon
my neighbor hits the bag
models skew
in central time

This morning "there came
to Aachen a curious sect"
who flooded the streets
in liege, in utrecht
during the plague

they danced
until they fell from exhaustion
right next to the bodies
of their friends, they called this
Tarantism or St. John's dance
don't you think, reminiscent of Duncan

Lovely their feet pound the green solid meadow
Lovely join we to dance green to the meadow

Cassandra says if I can't get
tested at least I can add
myself to the numbers

her idea being
myth
after many corrections
the tart cherry lozenge
lying down to piss in the shower
carrying the splintery bones of Pinocchio
in soft leathery bag

& light from the train window
flashes off your phone

telos is a feature
trix are for kids

Eclogue IV: Blood-Soaked Vision

Ants ladle bloodroot
and bees come in vain
and fox call it bloodwort
and guests lounge possessed
of whatever plague entombs
our adoration, rewatch

planet earth pray
please don't let this
dumbass fall
shining a head-
lamp on the tracks,
a narrow moon
sized gap for death
to squeeze thru. Did you

know the moon was flat? Some
turd thinks it less important
to wash your hands than
wrists, "a metaphor for re-
ductiveness," how rank
tenets are spread: odd fluid
pours out a flame, distinct
haters make their
categories known.
Cried Miss Nichols

all talk is of substance
yet these men
talk to no one! Or
nobody doubts you have

much to say young cognomen, it's just
your handwriting sucks
so it's hard to take you seriously

Meanwhile all the other Romans are
at the beach or
throwing Molotov cocktails

it's five o five
I think my therapist forgot our appointment
waiting for a phone call I watch the moths
lick the oak edges hard gold candy
and check my bank account

To renounce the future is
different than abstaining, twining
string round the wingtips
one day the earth
will be plush as a yoga mat
w/ rare shapes
of shriveled cactus
and my ear will coolly ooze
instructions won
and scholars gathered in agreement
what have you etc.
But for now

it's overbearing
w/ serrating debts
so I twill & floss
alone by a sink
where spiders live
in ungovernable
script giving off

aggressor vibes, shy
ambience of a
corridor spread over
miles of fields

Go about eating
tomatoes spider, do
your work inside me:
I'm an air plant
in a cup
in the bathroom.
I forget to flush my excrement
but mean to forget

A Is for Aegis

Each day at dawn I put the
  discolored buds in my ears
I meander the pathways
        perceive the daemon
        trying to lure the cat down the stairs
  with a frayed orange thread

        and so the morbid fantasy persists
          as though finding empty seats
        in a darkened theater

        sitting down to watch
        amongst the difficult perfumes
    the history of strife and
    the history of pleasure
        then loaf nearby just to pet
    the inconsolable mare

On the trail the lady said
        you looked so pretty in your pink hat
    against the poppies from a half mile away

    Well, what about *now*?

            Hole where the hoof plod
            Gap where the rent went

    A is for aegis, B for Bear-Sterns

        w/ each plunge of the rig
          into sworn-off waters

I prep the console
I sample the gels
    suckling weevil of fallible gains
        integrating the poll
            with the voter
        osier and ichor
                starburst, fingerling, don't

    forget the vanilla soy cream!
        In Virgil
        there is an understanding
    this kind of lyric continuity
            is the provision of militaries
                frogs deep
            in a throng of nettle

    Do you refer to the repugnance
of your forebears in the past
        or the present? Do you prefer
            treaty and breach
                or the attachment
            of riders? In my dream

    Kevin told me to read
        "He is your Saturn"
        a poem by John Wieners
    that as far as I can tell
        does not exist
                —all I know
            he said look for the poem
                that ends
            Bambino
                yr flute
        is safe with me

≠

Spiritude, tense specter, quasi-
flightless bird flowing
in lukewarm sea columns

Deliberation needs input—

Literally "sound dying down"

To equate silence with the worshipers

Honest mistake, I slipped
behind the snack counter
semi-sleep-stained, a memory
of meats being shipped
thousands of miles

To find you're well within the realm
of accident management

Put in the middle disc

Whose fault is premature licensure
in intense settings?

Whose faults are intense settings
tangentially accordant
in the common purview?

And such hell is not confined to the antipodes

Literally "dead flakes of sun"

To live unaware of payments
And making those payments

Solvency vs. Liquidity

> *This is called the "critical flicker-fusion frequency," or*
> *CFF—the frequency at which a flickering light begins*
> *to appear as a steady light.*
> —Audubon Society Newsletter

Having finally sold our boat to bidders

Having sped final approval to forge

The Missouri, the ballot box, the miles of pipeline

Intricate, the lip turns in, in, invokes the rose or hydrant

In, in this, in the bronze age of technocrats

Gravity generates a pungent analytic waft

There, solvent, on the sea's red edge

No one wants to see that shit

Age blank, buoyant, water lapping around his face and body

Dollar bills fluttering out an open window

Dozens of asylum seekers on a bridge

And still I wager the latent blueness of hills

And still I force-feed the gallinules

Show up to camp on my swagway

Then enter the tunnel with littlest friction

The way you swim absent-mindedly across a lake

To withstand Congress' worst acts by *writing* them

Welcome lads and whinnies to the pulp-removal process

Welcome to the process of becoming countrified

A brief conciliatory claim I make to myself

That the context harbors the query

Just as every man need a mantra

For which the rich get subsidies

In starlight, the rest of us boarding our appointed bus

Or, as in previous dominions, flung right over the city's bare
     edge

I begin with solemn exhortation

I begin by soaking in mimesis to soften the pores

I and myself considering the cyclical terms of the contract

Have you considered renting a room in the asterisk?

The whirling of washers, the dinging of dryers

In the following spreadsheet

Can you reconcile the pairs?

A series of decisions

Keeping voters up at night

A sprawling bank of servers

Plucking data from its stem

A terminal volley

Hewing an intermittent stream

I appreciate the sentiment

I think it's already being expressed

As another semblance in search of persons

Just say capital made me and to capital I shall return

My default thus far having been to remove myself

From precious suckling, from the intensity of coverage, from
    any clear role in life like vapor dispersing

Like, what else is new

I'll find an oak, I'll crunch some numbers, I'll refresh my
    browser

Peeling disaffected droves from our attendant delusions

In a daily state, or a market known

There's no fall except languor, no shock beyond guile

A surge of timecards floods the management platform

Snippets of weather, florets of cloud

Earned as a source, wrought as a kind

Lodged in my calculus a colloquy verbatim

The way you smooth a cap to prep for spikes

Refusal to be a part of the system

Is the system's principle maintenance

Refusal to remit and refusal to decree

Such being the gestalt calculus

Employed by member states

Bullet-riddled with suchness

At which point the river's just a streambed

A blend of breakfast cheeses and fragrant meats

At the first sign of thermal layers coalescing

I dot dot dot hit the deck

Locating several new feeds & streams

A mantle of alder and myrtle for the resident fauna

A towhee's crass spirit, then vireos, some higgledy finches

In the haunted dome-shaped aftermath

Can you make out woodlands?

Secured by jobs?

I see myself as a lake-builder and a line-setter

A grief-stricken void only snacking can manage

The way Love-heavy lineups open the perimeter respectably

You can't hold what was never your ground

And you can't teach verticality

That shit comes ingrained

Eclogue V: To Love to Redound

Groggy senators
gravelly turds
too much non-ergodic
grease on the wings

in North Dakota they go
onk-a-chonk
twice a year

If you channel misery
into a syrup Lindsey said
it will cheer you up

Caleb gave hibiscus
to a few of us on our way
out the door drunk

three days later we
dangerously shed that fur
making lefthand turns
the clang of seals

If you stack
all possible proteins
the length of a school bus

Paul suggests basking
in that pill-shaped glow

to pitch from the stretch
to love to redound

Crystal Geyser

I try to read the bluff
at the basin and bank
at the reef to sing the
countriest song the earth
avails *"and pencil it*
thence" on sandstone
I suppose just like
how it sounds. Remarkable
how much wind fleeces
a realm traces back
the stunted formation
"amphitheatrical," "ambrosia
in the rock," spires
cathedrals, an oblique resting place
to bask w/out import
End State Maintenance
by rule-of-thumb
I will sit as the form
of a person
sits, stationary, compleat
on *hoodooed* beach, reverie
by valence fixed

Have you ever seen an Arby's within
Subway within Chevron
without signage? Purportedly
what was Shady Acres
still is: standard compression
and relief, wing beat, and
in smaller font: *Thanks!* Knew
a dude carried mail put coffee
in a vase to coast
without expectation
Salina to La Sal
to a town called Grand Junction
full of benches
never made it
Place this blob
and forget it
and hope for the best from
abandon's inscriptions

Spooked a goose from the grain
and a white-throated wren
and a flicker in the tamarisk
sharpening its beak on the last
bit of red bark, that's some
one's job, to dig for what
feasibility there is, a buttery spread
of extenuation
called tailings
black compote
can fly

Lost form of embroidery
tills the wave
cold hands
no one believes
resemble books no one
believes *anything* he says
exaggeratedly rotating
on a "living" parade mount
of cows, the living
definition of perplexity, six
by the bank, ten on the hill
between honest glib and reckless toil
and when it's gone off
I'm too afraid to get close
collecting cartonite shards
a kind of orange ash
propensity avails

Granted phosphor not
withstanding a crosswind
blows any kind of toxin
back into town
to survey the slope
to settle the base
to charter the mounds
extend the hill
in a variety of pairs
dual plates of loaf
transform to potash
evaporating the leachate
in large iron pots
from sea came spring
magpies on a muddy
spit, motionless cows
"the tender unsown
increase in melons"
on a purely lyric level
I'm not sure what to call
geyser rock—you mean

Devonian shale?
I do mean sea
but, like, swale
the dying faithful
to its Western slope
and herself a treasure
house to its memories
to feed the horses
their customary pails
in relation to incidents
that irk and reveal, or refuse
the words, get clean
of perusal to mark
the speech inclination
of constant pause—is that
a midwinter bullfrog? Fourteen
year old lawyer marches down
a dirt road, what a dull life
in a bare branch
against a red cliff
of formless convenience
living lowers the land cost
jerks the pan level, both eagles
now stuck, the river shifts—

An hour later we run a long rapid and stop at its foot to
examine some interesting rocks, deposited by mineral springs
that at one time must have existed here, but which are no
longer flowing.

What Is the Seed Grail?

It's how all my poems start:
increasing tenets, provisional entries, quiet removal
of the root that
otherwise confines this
nth
to fields where it
nests a snicker's wrapper blows
through the grass. Recognize
it? To flip the pancake

or to fold it
to shift mitigation
my sense is he wants to avoid the subject
& pedals through birch
to a broad and semiotic
trench. Suffice we notice
the heat of the air,
the coolness of the surface
but nothing gnomic, no
bird with a crest.

Unaware Fiction

Unaware fiction
      was pictureless

    & mercury
    to be believed

no more paradigms, just
          spersing computation

    all over the tongue
until the tongue is destroyed

      Paul said clever,
    cake is an equation

        Prue: *I don't do math,*
            I never do math

if you live underwater
      but like feeling air

    salt helps
    sustain hallucination

        to not allow the self
        to touch the ground

I tried to listen only
      to sounds at a distance

I could sense whatever it was

slowly leaking from my ear

intolerable protein, dis
       continuous narrative

     why the adjective
            always outlast the noun

          Every week I receive the same
      enigmatic voicemail

     mister, you were covered from day one
     is now the time to pay up?

      I do I believe I was born
      but by what figment, sleuth

    when analysis lacks
  equivocation reigns

        I think if I had a child
      and that child wrote a poem

         amino, affidavit
      I used to think these were people's names

Lowest Common Denominator

I merely inhabit a preexisting niche

I pour one out for emolument

Jacuzzi in the squid's mantle

Guiding the aphid to its hangnail

A gross misunderstanding of freight

Should avoid the feed bargain

Shouldn't lift a finger to the lowly eye

Quiet, lightning-shaped, met with Augustus

To discourage all trotters from taking the court

Loquat-peppered, epical, pumped

Reach for the rabbit, don't pick up

Encomia

Pliny perceived earthworms
I see ash on the Prius

the less like the past
the future is

the more it takes
place in real time

daily pummeling growth
tedious ramping skyward

"the future that is
full of jobs for poets
at $90,000 per year"

first installment
and exhortation

Karin said it has to do with
the emulsifying of a shape

into figure
a process

of labor and sentiment
or music in war

Frontend Concept + Backend Design

Same difference, how the shrill
underwhelm the living

and what a day to sober up
between mats

a solid conclusion
coming back to me

like numerous alarms
in quality time

reprise yourself, concept
for thought removal

speaking in sentences
leveling entire provenances

it's hard to get comfortable
once exposed to the app

Eclogue VI: Automatic Cancellation

Sipping the aloe of partial
employment I unlock the hatch
back I discontentedly brim

a dog on its side
in the porphyry wilds

through me pass words
syntagms, waning
bits of formulae, what
Barthes calls densification
floating bereft & commensurate
like dumplings in a broth

it comes down to
whether you display an intent
on the road to the coliseum
I saw a lesser
god w/ its mouth full
almost a nymph

& like that I
like to put entire lines
into the search bar
to see what comes next

Unlicensed lyric
unlicensed gothic lyric
basically about Berkeley
California, the big trees
shaking with malware

and the vegan delicacies
of indigestible melon

& all the organisms onward crawling
to the bunkbeds that await
our ungratified sucking
at the foot of the bridge

Have you heard of turnspit dogs?
Small dogs that turned spits
of meat in the sixteenth century by
walking inside a wheel

The British loved to roast beef
like this
Linnaeus called them
canus vertigus, "the dizzy dog"

usually comments
burning skulls & epic reverberation

To be honest you're the
third trimmer to recommend me
that five-toed footwear

as in both instances of undertaking
I had hopes of singling out
what goes without saying

a little clause in my contract
little known, little liked

either clot or exude

The Middle Ages

From now on, everything will be called The Middle
—Lisa Robertson

So I lost my temper in the details
of a soft response to history
in the singular way
I could conceive it: dangling
like a bulb before me—by
which I took my vast
unsatisfying nap, my simple
leafy meal—tongue lolling
off the side of me, licking the
dew from the dents
in my purview—and mistook it
for a miracle, the middle
ages, the yearned-for
day boding an ambience
of homage, truly
careless, or so I

thought about it, a bounty
of attitudes and effects like
summer cumulus (now
seething, now spurned), now sky
like the people beneath it
unable to make up its mind,
the severity of the stigma silencing
the relativity of its decay.
So I mistook it for a miracle
unaware of the explanations
and protests, having already
started up the hill, having started

to detail the promiscuous
pairings: hormone and currency,
weather and dollar, time and
cash—making distinctions to no avail
in the middle ages—

how else turn blithe indication
into an action but tell it to rove?

So I operated under the pretense
of knowledge or emotion
in the middle ages
and learned to limp gravely
to feel particularly rueful
as though pinkening—to quiet down
in a plausible situation of gas—
naked in my aimlessness, protein
rich and polyp heavy
and deposited my money
like a mood, like mirth—my need
making a nest of want's
exhaustion, my intention bent

naturally as much as any
green stem. And so went
a large part of me running
backward through the middle
ages, jeweled with elision,
dissociating from a threshold,
the air so clearly marked from
charting redundancy among
urges, manufacturing whatever
fact fumes doxa, taking a few more
days of national coverage—

where's the repose in reckoning
with this squat audience of particulars?

So subsequence did not become
consequence as we thought, but
endless contestability, effervescent
evenings, abandoned structures
in the shape of disregarded
theories, the model I took
from a kind of combinatory
bird, the last legible force in the
middle ages, and labored upward
as the sparrow describes, making
maneuvers that informed my route,
speaking in subtle statements about

departure yet with fewer and fewer
reasons to leave the room, I passed
lightly through that reactionary
darkness, a bee stuck by
single thread
to its
erstwhile politic
and recognized this sinking
action as the long-awaited function
of green, and this agitation
as a mist settling round
pillars, or the middle
ages, its bridge—

Horace

ab ovo usque ad mala

Beach grasses, backache, wobbling gulls
      rain clouds, cypresses that seem heroic—

Virtually every mouth itches
      in this assembly of peregrines, fumbles
for coinage, leafing through lavender
      the entire flat realm over,
a deli sandwich you can run your
      cold hand across, beefing up roosts
in corporate woody dew. Say we dwell
      in Oakland—can this port city wrest
but credit of labors
      having spirally flecked from in
credulous heavenly rung? O rented
      Earth, scattered rotunda, scarce shelter
of geese and squirrels, mopeds, colony
      collapse, upon which I cask my spigot
muse "whose seedpods
      came over as packing
for Chinese porcelain" though each
      time I turn the faint wren
disperses! Still nothing
      compares to the asterisk
shaped lake in the middle of
      summer, sad but true, en route
to the ocean, slight tilt of the head
      to the surf, widening
fan-like, adolescent, bobs its heads
      from the waves. Fuck
cops and lobbyists, it's not

too sonorous to say?? The rest will follow
these ribbons of youth until
                gone by noon, pulled
trinket, dull flux, still getting to
                know my family better, "from the eggs
to the apples," which is
                what it means in Latin.

I Make the Loose Tooth Friends

Substitute a buoyant
dereliction of traces
whose outward curve is
bound for resentment, the long
nameless European vine
calling in to contemplate the
verities, Jared in Fremont, Jared
what u got? Came
from the burb, marred by the vortex
you have to begin speaking in order
to be ordained, solid non
voter out there in the
open woods. Leg asleep
in a car loaded with bikes
going to the coast
the sacrum's true destroyer
bullet points the day
as spam sinks the bucket
intelligence questions
the signifier for heaven
a lack of discernible wills.
Not your typical montage
rain drifting with fatherly
disregard, I seek a form of
daisy literally *in* the grasses,
a dispassion for perfidy,
the figure for which is
the oxygenated brain.

Eclogue VII: Hack Your Life

Hack your life or vie
w/ constant boarding
a referee's body
Entering Tuesday

I hear the soft beguiling bells
of San Francisco, the city of
rich malcontents and
emblematic ringing
of liberal atonement
and discarded terraces

Hollywood warbler crossing
a dozen freeways

I cross the bridge
with subtle expectations
I keep to myself

Insurrection as a mutual thirst
responsive to plumes
bell pepper & peas

Suspicious entreaty
dijon on your jacket
on your puffy Patagonia jacket

Who over the age of ten
likes to wear crowns?

Whoso the bell of wantonness
doth clang against its ledge?

City Lights

Joan Murray, drafts
and fragments, Norma's
new book, Swedish songs
translated to English
someone yelling *no*
signal! in the middle
of the road a bright yellow
byrd gets crushed by a lyft

Maybe it happens once a month
you leave your lair
beneath thickening clouds
& harrowing leaves
to feel the friction
of the choices you've made
to conspire or follow

choices that lead
to notice of removal
or approval
way, way out
in all this chromatic sun
or when it was
behind clouds
and everlasting thought

It's like the troubadours say
"richer tunes bring greater follies"
take the mockingbird yapping
in persistent wind
like a misshapen wave

prone to inquiry
pours down knowhow
never ending

our boss told Ben
it sings so many songs
bc it is the bird lacking love

Rapidly Reversible Tattoo

There I was
learning to work it
hushing the stigmas
salvaging hope as a dialogue

as recently dissected
to feed the needs of the jolted
When you leak it
you know

salvaging stacks as a dialogue
tending the desiderata
w/ heirloom eyes
in equal parts levelheadedness

and privy onus
afloat on the Yuba
the kind of pitching
that yields to fielding

and there I was
casually addled
on any bench
salvaging rates as a dialogue

as recently as yesterday
was that flake
had my lunch near shores

Arrival

The grass reaches up overhead and braids its faint dream
with the horizon. The earth's lengths, the sky's tread have
been miscalculated, or otherwise exaggerated. Clouds
sharpen on the hillsides, monikers dropped. Bluebird, a
budding sequence, albeit retractable, signifies a sort of
hovering in place. Sun, stars, equator, azimuth. Turtles
spawn in the sewage ponds. It's hard to describe the gravity-
less chamber. Desire flakes inside it. Future-threshold-
cum-sudden-conveyance. The moment we enter, the body
reorients around this deafening new principle. Italics?
Remember, we are parallel to earth, gathering our thoughts,
afraid to inch forward. The apparatus needs input; the input
needs signage. Subtle intention has a way of obscuring
the obvious. I am a small ponderous mechanism. Seated
beside the module. The being awakes, startled. The future
answers by roughly lowering the shades. Life and death
expand in a series of rotating circles; it's unclear which is
the innermost—also, which the outer. Entry prefigures its
strain on the imagination. Scenes on earth seem rushed in
comparison.

Goodnight Moon

Triggered by bowel movements, and a pigeon's balmy
strain, I arrived around midway, on the night in question,
with perverse tendency toward description, my boss calls
it reckoning, an impediment to vestment, as the situation
defuels, now beachcombing's prodigious, a man making pig
gestures, with outline of indebtedness, and diamond of nines,
whilst I follow this Virgil, word travels from the electorate, I
ready the epinephrine, no one's here necessarily, the first five
knocks are Oscar, I motion to surrender, over a dense range
of particulars, only it's not really an allele, and these aren't
sugars for the baby, and the rut isn't shrinking, intoxicated
by the perennials, I shirk the very stakeholders, maintenance
retrieves the radish, don't let Daedalus on the couch, we
need to know what Exxon knew when they knew it, so we
can prove truth is an outlier, it's still frozen in parts, they
asked for house, I gave them house, large pods are amassing,
wildfires rage in Central Sweden, the laurel speaks of reprisal,
to discern the chronology of joyrides, I cozy up with some
gel-packs, making brief overtures to the gods, as the future
alters the finite, so our focus lately has been on softening
the blow, looping the gap between parallels, I'm just saying
check out the webbing, typically films keep something of their
scent, the core concept is downfall, I call this landscape the
shifting baseline, the crochet reef around the pubis, lupines in
abundance, the wasp larva digests a hole through the cuticle
of an aphid, and suddenly your tomato optimism dissipates,
and you're back to bombing, Verizon storefronts, emerging
dugways, I zoom in on the ancients, great strength needs
eclogues, all the realists are hibernating, say you move to get
health care, the sixth knock is Sherry, there are stones in my
soup, just budget the length of our stay.

Antiquity and Onomatopoeia

for Norma Cole

All April have
that same dream
sinking feeling as of water
into an onyx shell

I get emotional
we're moving
masturbate on my chest
then shower

situational text
mirrored wake
in the fog

huge boughs
of forgotten walnut
confused heart
"as patient as pearl"

the amount sprayed is equivalent
to spreading 2¾ tablespoons
of liquid over a football field,
she said, or 7½ thimblefuls

dream you
see you
tell you
(this)

*

Night, the
price increases
echelon, agapanthus

swift as any influence
barbaric anthems
beginning to erase footprints
"examining the heavens"
At this point
books are not phones, yet

Fall, framboise, buttering
toast, anonymous calls
lessons to be learned
the transformation from
green to pink to gray

Spring,
lay in bed: sun, traffic, cat
quiet, door opening
against carpet, routine
movements become

laden, suggestions

*

Actors
reading books
they've dramatized
sitting against a blue background

librarian

walks into a bar and asks
how'd they make animal sounds
in ancient Greece?

Just combine
the relevant search terms
antiquity and onomatopoeia

*

Raise your hand
if you keep facing the walls
with batteries in bags
& fuel from shells

an egg sashaying on
human legs, a spoon
stuck in its broken top
and a pig rooting for
acorns with a slice of
ham cut from its
back, the knife
invitingly left there

a Flemish fable that
if you eat your way
through a mountain
of gruel you come to
a land where ham and
eggs eagerly await, and
geese fly already roasted
into your open mouth

and you're not alone

Eclogue VIII: No-Filter Malfeasance

CREF year comes exec
at the drying edges of a lake
dead last in reps
self-care is the beta

My lord works through subpoena
said "probe the Hyatt"
and brought me to a little knoll
of discounted herbs

Dreamt of workouts for depression
stoked to be honest
in tautological displeasure
w/ soft tissue enflamed

check out the moon's
no-filter malfeasance
I can't repeat each decree
of the framed night's rotation

Usually
when you spill in the waterway
hanged bells in skulls
spotted a ray in the lake

Telluric

Fawns and beasts dance
to good music. Oaks sway,
flies find the inside
of cups. A centurion is said to have
punched Virgil, who called
the cops. "The young radical
who becomes a supporter of
existing institutions." Dabbles
in cosmogony. Gets Horace
paid, too. Were friends
warning him to not
become a tool? Yeah, I have
been paid by the state at
times in my life: to clean
equipment at the gym, teach
kids, check in and out
books. Never
              that much. And not to
be a poet. These days
that work is done by
trolls and pundits—listen
closely to the curses they cast.
Minor colds, daily spells,
inventions of likeness
and musical dissonance,
all these make the placebo
perfect, mere
              ambiance dissolving
into blue flickers of sensitivity
until the indoctrinating eye
of the eclogue
concentrates elsewhere.

Cynics were the original
epicureans. Some say
the eclogue was devised
by Theocritus in the third
century almost out of
whole cloth. Others trace it
back to the Homeric Hymns
of an earlier phase: cool grass,
thin air—the
                    alpine flowers
on Ricola Originals. Did
beauty come first or does
wealth? Every so often a
telluric daze falls over the world
like a key change, predictable
yet hazardous in its staggering
conviction. Lips turn purple
from some fugitive coat
of sugar: speech, bloodred,
etchings of amaryllis.

Flat Earth Theory

There is a joke most annulments
don't curtail expectations, or pertain
to these, or that but backward, as
basic force of habit enters under
water worlds of rags & sponges
you'll be surprised to learn no
model conducts first. Let them forever
say I did better as a listener
receding in habitude, left
to the professionals, laughing
when you laughed, out
canceling pairs. Brittle
as the leaf peels, diagnosis
does make a stern fate of apparatus
some expert overheard the effects
resemble that kind of minding
that comes at a cost—

I conduct a surface
skated-on or sounded-out,
I stand in the water like I were
truly semiotic. So what does happen
when my understanding defeats
its purpose, cognition separated
into blast radius and coagula
has an effect on the butterflies
who nibble and chew on the scurf?
As discrepancy is a rhythm
each industry has its litmus that
that person is assigned to directly—

do I call it my hard drive?
The use of such throttle
provides gradual pressure
against a mistake-laden matrix
lacking an apparent sequence
my curiosity is with cursory
retention—*I left the pool when
I was told to*—a patient's ability
to note the same span backward.
That facility itself says fuck
norms, do you know what form
you'd prefer for your portrayal?
For context helps me
remember to turn the oven off,
living adaptively in the know-

how of not ruling things out, identifying whole
guilds marching upward
unto the melted horn.
Now what does that mean?
Good question. In this case
seeking is a form of
address meant to
input the attention such as
donning and doffing a jacket
versus the neurotypical population
I prefer the mustering of aspects
to provide a sort of shadow
support under the impatient canopy
of clarification. An example would be the phrase
the people of Java would like to sue the company
and the company would like to sue
the earth. It's radar diagnosis. Rather
indictment. A leisure skill is

basically something you're exposed to, not
not happening on a particular weekday
whilst going to the threshold to
say things you never really grip
the meaning of. For one to
automatically turn the page I store this as
sensation which needs revisiting,
a side of the street with poorly
drawn signage, missing the point at which
a mistake would be clarifying
I proceed with confidence
at a rate of fluidity
going back to notice this
me is consistent with the concept
of annealing. Go ahead. Leave a message.

Permian Disappearance

All night
    you add knowledge to the marsh
  and lavish the wrist with coats
to protect against loose
        polarity

    I rush along the pathway coated with retractions
    Give me the brisk attainment—

        you mean Brisk, the
        Lipton Iced Tea?

      Never doubt
    as praise the
      signal contortion
  moving potted plants

      to melt the bonds
    the defining feature of a spectrum
    I beckon the founder

   the desert is huge
     argyle patterns on moss

There has to be more to this game than reversals

All night
    the idea of my severe and resilient image
  flickers on a few dark windows

The first task is to exit the landscape

caught
wiping down a fridge—

Kevin, Come Back

The creamiest sun rises and sets over
San Francisco, the city I can see out
my bedroom window, scattered w/ undies
and socks
and the pink jacket that's
good to wear on the windy edge of a lake
on Mission and 3rd
that's good to wear to meet you in front of the museum
to go get naked at a dead poet's grave

like when my friends and I
used to go streaking through the
Salt Lake cemetery, land of that punk
with blue hair, high up
where an ancient lake left
crooked lines on the hill
undressing and ogling ourselves a bit like
Hostess pastries before they get all smushed

and higher up turning
my head out the plane window
to see Mt. Shasta, Wintu
holy site others believe
is filled with Lemurians
one and a half million of them actually
much taller than us and full of
disdainful platitudes yet residing
in buttery, crystalline peace
like humanoid croissants

and even higher up
I think I can see the street
you live on, Minna, just kidding
I can't, not even with binoculars
I can only see the troublesome outline
of that technocratic utopia where helicopters
swirl the air to soft-serve
and the youngest looking people pretty much
have all the money
and fog oozes like in the second
Ninja Turtles, *Secret of the Ooze*
tho I can't remember the secret
I know you would

Eclogue: Reprise

Daphnis, no, I don't
want to know what love is
but I bet we've already
been exposed. Love is life
to the max, all the pain
and sorrow, wired through
cables, cybernetic and
extensible, across the flowering
field and below the boisterous
sea. Love is like carbon
entering the Arctic vault
tons at a time, befouling
seas, taking vengeance
on earth, dumping all this
material here theorists muse
over and we labor under
between dissent and decree
like some ahistorical ploy
so cruel in its conference
as the black oak up
the tall ponderosa
climbs, plumbs
but never more
than halfway. Bound
by these untenured shoots
I fume in my madness
a dizzied squirrel, hating
birds, getting poked
by pine and ignored
by thrush whose song
gives glands the time

they need to make
the goosebumps
I wish upon no one
else. Echo, psyche*!!* The
data is bad: I'm afraid
nothing is real and
description is pointless
yet I feel it in my heart, a
raging fire whose fuel
I cannot find, pure
torture at any temperature
like frozen peas suddenly
brought to a boil—I guess
I will depart and re-
tune the songs it should
suffice your poet to
have sung. Ugh. First noon
now night, snuck aloft, now
look, just look at me biting
my fingers until they come
off. Twice in the past
I don't know, maybe
months, I've had
to go to the nearest
hospital and explain
how pathetic I am as
they drain the puss
from the nail. Why love
is it like this*??* You've mined
the pit of my soul and
life's frayed swivel speaks
to this. My friends
tell me not to draw connections

but my philosophy blasts
their contentions to shit
and tokes remaining schwag
endowing me with
poisonous faith and
unfavorable karma
and blasts their words
to silt that chokes once
amazing brooks—no more sienna,
emerald—to the north
and south. Now all realms
suck*!!* That's enough my best
friend says, but even
her voice sinks into the
contaminated pit so
treacly and treacherous
a family of geese lands
only to wither quickly
into mush. And to think
in flight they'd have been
a wedge or skein*!!* Me, I can't
even think that hard, don't have
wings to fold, forlorn, my skin is
dead hair in a wreath and all
stained are my clothes. These
sandals don't fit. Or maybe
they do, just love turns every
inch to shit. Are the lights all
off*??* Please let me circle this
drain in the dark. I can't see
into the future, at least
there's that, though I'm
terrified of what love will

do next. Pound down the door
while I'm strewn on the couch,
plug up my ass, playing
porn or solitaire on the phone
I carry with me like an
impenetrability charm.
I have to remind myself
you, hey, the one that looks
like an awkward figure eight,
with supplicant face of wax
when applied, whatever
catches your attention doesn't
pass for transcendence—you
were not designed in a lab
at Stanford. Of course, a friend
later tells me this is logically
inconsistent and she's right, I always
get ekphrasis and analog wrong.
Everyone says I'm too negative
to be loved but I say I
deserve it more. I can list
the names of birds and trees
what else would a true
love want?? Before I used to be
so abstract in my horror
at the world's affairs, a fellow
beachgoer and mellow
Greek—now I'm that asp who
strikes feet in the street to notify
them of the nature of empire.
It truly is that bad. My song
is like radioactive decay
forever breaking down but

never going away. And me
and my love are those
two lines always approaching
but never to touch.*!!*

Eclogue IX: Microfiche

Often permitted to
walk out of work with
a tray full of pastries

the scaly fish come forward
exhibit the antonym
effort of the lungs

Shores smacking
in decked-out headspace
nominal goons
rose-scented wigs

say bye to the raiders
bye to the dubs
enter the city of your choice
through knee-high grass

At times I emerge
a vulture vexed by the pursuit
of a habitat to frequent
a large polemical star

Dying, like eating
through inedible leaf—methinks
a mildewed apiary
covered with ants

& bubbles rising
from the bottom of my intention
a metaphor for whatever
climbs out of my mouth

Deep Space Ballot

Visualize the abutment
collecting meter-change
in some sort of raised-bed futurity
this vehicle is for human mourning
I can see clear through the rear chamber
hidden somewhere in
green eyeliner
the voting populace
treasure the grebe
its rancorous salute
& topped-off parfait
which flower blossoms first
in this adjusted scenario
we were enjoying something of a sip
a Sunday ceasefire
what's a parrot doing on that ramekin?
a parrot on that ramekin
with fingers as on a keyboard
slide your money under the sculpture
why there, under the sculpture?

Direct Deposit
for Alli Warren

I can't hear the song repeating

sun rising as thru the stem of the apple

I can't sponge the rook or transplant the gulls

can't in part due to public sentiment

can't between primarily economic poles

even when I wreck the badge

I can't fool the starlings

nor epoxy the wheels

can't guarantee a seat

or tariff the plow

Still I can't excuse it

I can't get any closer to it

can't reenact my own absence

were it mine to reenact

Burdensome Organ

Then Luther nails up his list of confessions

with nothing on it.

Then the fiefdoms flood

with daily estimation and nightly shortcoming.

Then the land falls asleep in the water,

thousands say their skin is pricked,

then autumn, carnage, then monuments.

Then the clouds turn white with concept.

Then a box comes in the mail

labeled unintended consequences.

Then again could be a list of concessions.

Still, it has nothing on it.

Canto

Foresight imagines a basic recollection of death.

Tumors in the face, lungs, kidneys and breasts.

Hold the spirit at a distance.

How long does each world last?

The tree may take a certain shape.

The farmer claims a certain tax exemption from the state.

I start crunching the numbers and a foreboding prism
    appears.

I listen to the wind as I walk down the hill.

Is this tree like that one, these walls a house still?

Entire solemn lives lived in the grasses...

Peeling wax from an ear until it bruises...

I'm watching you watching the game unfurl.

What kind of thing is this person telling me?

What kind of thing is this tree?

Eclogue X: Dunk On My Face

Figure out the animal, flush the remnants
forgive the lacuna
its constant pluralizing

As with any continuous loss of flavor
the root conceals
grave efficacy
to the founder's intent

& what about privation
means to have warned the body
of sordid sympathies,
rugged impasto

Damned in our free time
Damned to whet the lordless trove

that makes leagues of us
highlighting film's mechanics,
living proof kite is a kind of bird

and like a face about to speak
I, speaker, stomach provisions

early summer rains drag on
young boys in blue life jackets
my bias inherent to the data

The Deserts of Saturn

If this is it folks, well I still
feel the need to make
everything relate to the
Eclogues. Sitting under the low
low slope of sun like
a litmus did you know
what scatological is? I
didn't. I was
listening to this
podcast about struggle & how
we all laughed. A very American
class of laugh. I wasn't
even alive but I'm sure I
laughed. We millennials
are the worst. Actually
I have a letter from
Bill Clinton telling me to
keep it up! The king of
creeps. Thumbs up. Years later

wandering the deserts of
Saturn, Diane said
your poetry is so
scatological. Bent over
in search of a policy
for what the gods tell me—
the horrible gods with their
excellent kettles. Bent over
a toilet the guy in
the next stall asks
how do you cancel this

goddamn subscription?
On the wall between us
someone had scrawled

HELL IS A PENDULUM

followed by the warning

SPOILERS = INSTANT BAN

I thought maybe that's
scatological? Scatterbrained
pacing, empty
stares. "This isn't
shit, it's poetry," says
Camille Roy. The rain
started last night
and someone punched
me in the head trying
to steal my laptop.
I woke in pain. "Shit enters
it only as an image." The proof
is right fucking there. Mopsus said Daphnis
taught mankind to yoke in cars.
Rachael said the neighbor's
need to deal with the rain
water on their roof. But I guess
it was only a dream. And it's with
great difficulty I rise
from bed and try
the next eclogue:

        Coach said
        No dweller in verdure

can appreciate my sorrow
being governed by wings
who can't shoot the three
like backing
your car into traffic
with little regard
comes everlasting avoidance

Earthquake in Alaska
"downhill" reactions
N-95 masks
running to the market
dashing to the market
to watch the boy
carve fantastically
underneath a tarp

Coach yelled explain
yourself, explain why you
don't like karaoke
you little shit

Actually I kinda do!
When Virgil wrote the
Eclogues he was definitely
going through his Saturn
return. Now what? This morning
you left the door open and
I dreamt I went to synagogue
for the first time in years.
Someone stormed in
grabbed the cup &
threatened to spill it right
there on the scrolls. Honestly how

trite I thought, that's
already been done. It's
already been done I
thought but not
in the eclogues.

ACKNOWLEDGMENTS

I feel unfathomable gratitude to Evan Kennedy and Dirty Swan Projects for publishing the spine of this manuscript in a chapbook version of *Mine Eclogue*; to MC Hyland, Anna Gurton-Wachter, and Jeff Peterson at DoubleCross Press for publishing many of these poems in the chapbook *A Is For Aegis*; to Sophia Dahlin for your exuberance for and dedication to these poems, as if they were your own; to Eric Sneathen for an early reading that steered the manuscript; to Jean Day, Brian Blanchfield, and Brandon Brown for your generous blurbs and continuous engagement with my writing; to Francisco Fenton, who translated versions of these poems for the *Salón de Belleza* reading series at Aeromoto in Mexico City; to Justin Carder for your wild and exacting design, and for always being game to collaborate and make BIG things happen; and to David Wilson, a favorite Bay Area artist, for your brilliant cover art.

Thanks to Caleb Beckwith, Kate Robinson Beckwith, Caren Beilin, Roberto Bedoya, Alan Bernheimer, Amy Berkowitz, Lindsey Boldt, Joseph Bradshaw, Julian Talamantez Brolaski, Turner Capehart Canty, Matt Carney, John Coletti, Paul Ebenkamp, Ivy Johnson, Andrew Kenower, Nate Klug, Sara Larsen, j.j. Mull, Michael Nicoloff, Steve Orth, Bob Perelman, Kit Schluter, Violet Spurlock, Jamie Townsend, Diane Ward, Alli Warren, Laura Woltag, and the late great Kevin Killian— your own work and friendship were instrumental.

Thanks to *Lana Turner* (Calvin Bedient & David Lau), *Mirage #5 Period(ical)* (Dodie Bellamy & Kevin Killian), *Elderly* (Jamie Townsend & Nicholas DeBoer), *grama* (Meagan Wilson), and *MARY: A Journal of New Writing* (Emily Alexander) for publishing versions of these poems. And to the editors, translators, and publishers of the collection, *Salón de Belleza*

(Gato Negro Ediciones/Wolfman Books), for anthologizing the 70+ poets from all over the world that read in the series.

Lastly, thanks to my family and to Karin Dahl for everything and otherwise—love you!

Author photograph *by* Karin Dahl.

JACOB KAHN is a poet and editor living in Oakland, CA. He is the author of the chapbooks *A Is For Aegis* and *Mine Eclogue*, and *A Circuit of Yields: A Handbook for Giants*. From 2016–2020, he was a managing editor, curator, and bookseller at Wolfman Books, a bookstore, small press, and community arts hub in downtown Oakland. He is an editor of the poetry chapbook press, Eyelet Press, and reading series, Islet, which he cofounded with Sophia Dahlin in 2019. He works as a freelance grantwriter and copyeditor, as well as at the Berkeley Public Library.

ROOF BOOKS

the best in language since 1976

Recent & Selected Titles

- SCISSORWORK by Uche Nduka, 150 p. $20
- THIEF OF HEARTS by Maxwell Owen Clark, 116 p. $20
- DOG DAY ECONOMY by Ted Rees, 138 p. $20
- THE NERVE EPISTLE by Sarah Riggs, 110 p. $20
- QUANUNDRUM: [i will be your many angled thing]
  by Edwin Torres, 128 p. $20
- FETAL POSITION by Holly Melgard, 110 p. $20
- DEATH & DISASTER SERIES by Lonely Christopher, 192 p. $20
- THE COMBUSTION CYCLE by Will Alexander, 614 p. $25
- URBAN POETRY FROM CHINA editors Huang Fan and
  James Sherry, translation editor Daniel Tay, 412 p. $25
- BIONIC COMMUNALITY by Brenda Iijima, 150 p. $20
- QUEENZENGLISH.MP3: POETRY: Poetry, Philosophy, Performativity,
  Edited by Kyoo Lee, 176 p. $20
- UNSOLVED MYSTERIES by Marie Buck, 96 p. $18.95
- MIRROR MAGIC by John Sakkis, 96 p. $18.95
- I AM, AM I TO TRUST THE JOY THAT JOY IS NO MORE OR
  LESS THERE NOW THAN BEFORE by Evan Kennedy, 82 p. $18.95
- THE COURSE by Ted Greenwald & Charles Bernstein, 250 p. $20
- PLAIN SIGHT by Steven Seidenberg, 216 p. $19.95
- IN A JANUARY WOULD by Lonely Christopher, 90 p. $17.95
- POST CLASSIC by erica kaufman, 96 p. $16.95
- JACK AND JILL IN TROY by Bob Perelman, 96 p. $16.95
- MOSTLY CLEARING by Michael Gottlieb, 112 p. $17.95
- THE RIOT GRRRL THING by Sara Larsen, 112 p. $16.95
- THOUGHT BALLOON by Kit Robinson, 104p. $16.95

Roof Books are distributed by
SMALL PRESS DISTRIBUTION
1341 Seventh Street • Berkeley, CA. 94710-1403.
spdbooks.org

Roof Books are published by
Segue Foundation
300 Bowery #2 • New York, NY 10012
For a complete list, please visit **roofbooks.com**